FB

Sky Girl

rosemary griggs

Cover illustration by   John Murphy*
Author Photo by   A. Friend

Published in the United States by

Fence Books
303 East Eighth Street, #B1
New York, NY 10009
212-674-0199
fence@angel.net
www.fencebooks.com

Book design by   Fence Books

Distributed by   University Press of New England
www.upne.com

Library of Congress Cataloguing in Publication Data
Rosemary Griggs [1973–]
Sky Girl / Rosemary Griggs

Library of Congress Control Number: 2003112521

ISBN 0-9713189-8-0

First Edition

*I would like to thank my parents and siblings, my teachers, Neal
Salogar, and everyone who contributed to bringing this book together.*

*John Murphy is a sculptor and cartoonist with an affinity for imagi-
nary creatures. He works in the San Francisco Bay area as a freelance
illustrator and manufacturer of a line of stuffed toys made from old
socks. These "Stupid Creatures" can be seen at www.stupidcrea-
tures.com. Murphy proliferates these Creatures in the popular culture
as toys, comic books, and animated works. He can be contacted at
murphy@stupidcreatures.com.

Printed in Canada by Westcan Printing Group

For the crewmembers lost on September 11, 2001.

And for my grandmothers.

Contents

III. Recovery

I.   *Satellite* derives from the Latin word for *attendant*

Saginaw

Kimberlie in her little
room again peck peck
pecking at the carpet.
Are there cracker crumbs or nail
polish chips—no.
Laughter in the next room
making her sad.
Should be happy people are
happy. Should be Kimberlie.

The monitor humming and the clock
and the light. Linoleum. Saturday.
Shadows passing under the door.

No one will come don't be
afraid if they do smile like
you love them people
like that.

Kimberlie trying not to take life
seriously sits on the plastic couch.
She's an object in the room
and scatters her things about:
suitcase, shoes, overcoat.
She feels a little bit better.

Sky Girl

I could I could be so big I could take up the whole page or hover in the corner and you wouldn't even see me but you'd know I was there because I would be everywhere even under the bed.

at night the fairies come out to protect you you
shouldn't be afraid you should lie down like a good girl
but I would turn out the light so the people
outside won't see you

I could be on the news or the moon I would rise to the surface of your soup I'd be who you always wanted me to be who my mother wants me to be who I want to be.

I didn't say someone was outside for sure

I don't know I was suggesting

I realized one day I was small. My clothes were made for children and the high doorframe only a courtesy to my guests. That is a lie: I would like to make them bend down. The arch is high to suggest heaven. In case anyone is there, hovering, watching me because they like me. I can still swing. I can fit on the Sit n' Spin.

BOS-ORD

Basically, it breaks down like this: if every thought we have and everything we experience is recorded in our bodies, in our genes, and we pass our genes down to our children and so on, then it is possible that your body remembers the lives of your ancestors—it's in the genetic makeup—which could account for past life experiences.

Is that true?

It's a theory.

I'll bet that's true.

Sharon Tate Anonymous

Kimberlie, Kimberlie, and Marie
meet to promote recovery.

in the little white house
it's often raining
spoiling the chocolate cake

Kimberlie presents her painting:
a pregnant woman hanging.
She's wearing a beautiful dress,
says Marie, *Is that what she was*
really wearing?

one rain drop falls
on Marie's eyelash she
finishes her chocolate cake

The bare, bronze feet are dangling.

Friendly Employees

The handsome young first officer comes out of the cockpit to help Kimberlie say goodbye to the passengers,

Okay, now, if it is someone you would sleep with say, "Have a good day." I'll do the same.

HKG-SFO

Claudio with tripod and camera
followed by *I go by Chrissy*

Carrying sticks and ribbon one by one in her mouth
it's most difficult in the beginning the balancing.

She sings men frequent her here eventually
one will stay depending:

contribution is proportional to certainty,
as the photos will prove.

This picture of my first baby,
she my good luck.
I'm glad I had a girl most Chinese
don't want girl
but girls stay close to home
and boys go out in the world.
If I had a boy I would have to try again
and I don't want another baby it hurt too much.
They made me stay in hospital 5 extra day
you know some women kill their baby
every time they ask me how I feel I just
start crying and can't stop I don't know.

The One

I never called because you're crazy. You made the whole thing up in your head and left the party. I never cheated on you. If anything you should apologize to me.

Cocoa

Hamsters make good pets for children because they are cute and small and are relatively easy to take care of. It is a good way to teach a child about responsibility as the hamster will need fresh food and water each day. Also, because hamsters only live about 2 to 3 years, it is a good way to teach your child about death.

Phuket January 2000

Around the outside of the fruit her fingers slip.
A monkey sleeping on the wall awakens
and knocks his nails against his teeth.
She thinks it is her sister calling from the room.

Siamese cats thought they were more beautiful than God
so their tails were broken.
Now all cats' tails are broken and the dark green foliage
brushes her wet hair.

She turns the corner of the temple
mud between her toes, salt taste,
she feels incredibly clean. Flash of light
to the right an old white man
photographs the young girl lying in the mud
fingers laced behind her head
bikini laugh breast.

Inside the house now lungs hurting
from the space from the cigarettes.
Pink bougainvillea around her sister's neck
in the yellow light the whirling fan.
They want me to shoot razor blades out of my vagina now.
I'm not sure I want to try that.

Phuket January 2000

Have you seen the children carrying caged birds?

The idea is you'll give them money and they'll let the bird go.
It's supposed to bring you good luck.

One kid approached me the other day. I put my hand on my
stomach and shook my head, *Oh no thank you son, I've just
eaten lunch.*

The boy was very frightened.

Poem for Cecil

He keeps a journal in the backseat which passengers write in.
He gets jokes and phone numbers,
Cecil likes to flirt.

But he thinks the windshield is a magnifying glass
on all the assholes in the city.
Sometimes he doesn't like how he's treated
but then sometimes he gets head so it all evens out.

Cecil has his ex-wife's name
mixed with the colorful snakes and drums
that cover his arms and chest.
It's like having sex with a painted sculpture or a reptile.
I am in love with Cecil.

We haven't spoken for two months and I try not to notice cabs.
Sarah doesn't know what I see in him
but the buff transvestite does.

Cecil wants to be an actor.
Cecil was in a play.

Isoka, a northern province of Zambia, 1999

People have been on the moon, he said. I said you're lying. It's true, he said. There is even an American flag up there. They think one day people might live there. They can't live there, I said. He said why not. I said, there isn't any grass—they couldn't build houses. What would they live in? And not only that, there isn't any millet or animals—what would they eat? They'd have to bring food with them from here I suppose. How—I said—How did they even get there? In a rocket, he said. A big plane that shoots straight up into the sky and goes to the moon. And they have to wear special suits because the moon doesn't have enough gravity or oxygen, so people float like they're in a big tub of water. I've never been in a big tub of water, I said. I don't know what it feels like to float. He said, one day if you get to the sea, go in the water and you will know what it feels like to be on the moon. I didn't believe him either. I laughed. You white people are funny, I said.

Then I started to think about it. If I was on the moon, what would the earth look like? Would I be able to see you smiling by your hut in your yellow dress? And I realized that I don't ever want to go to the moon. I don't ever want to leave here. What kind of people are these? I don't want them to come here anymore. You aren't helping us, I said. You're a white man, if you really want to help us, why don't you go to the capital, make money at one of those machines, and bring it back here. I know you can do it, I said. I know someone who has seen you do it.

Girl Talk

I knew who it was. I asked her if anything happened. I said please tell me I won't be mad at you but I need to know as a girl to a girl please help me out here. She said nothing happened.

Losing Julie

It rained, she says, watching the tires
smear on the street.
The rings of mascara under her eyes—
we woke up on 7th and Folsom.

All day I've been braiding her hair.
All day the sky's been dark
and no one passing says a word.
No one is listening.

I tell her my arms are tired.
I tell her that time she found the rabbit
nailed to the wooden gate—
I did it.
She doesn't care.

She has a drink in her left hand,
a braid in her hair.

Cinnamon

If he senses danger, the firemouth fish will hold his fry in his mouth until the danger passes.

The female hamster will also do this with her babies. However, the babies will suffocate in her mouth if she doesn't find safety soon enough. So if you are watching them in a cage, you can't stand there for too long.

SFO-DEN

August 3, 2001

I've flown with you before.

>   Yeah?

You're always at least 10 minutes late
and you can see people's energies.

>   That's right. You must
>   have a good memory.

How did you learn to see energies?

>   I was able to ever since I was a child.
>   My mom thought something was wrong
>   with my eyes. She took me to all kinds
>   of doctors.

How has that helped you? What
has that ability taught you?

>   I know we're here to be good to each
>   other and take care of each other.
>
>   A lot of people don't know that.

Confirmation

Heidi called from LA. *You were right,* she said, *my friend was at the party.*

He had way too much attitude for a man who was balding at his age anyway.

Give him ten years.
His attitude will change completely.

Nina

sexy tattooed blond
ex-wife of professional skateboarder

You look the way I felt after my husband left
me. We never talked about it either.

Betrayed by even my own self-image.

You should get a pet. My therapist told me
I should get a pet.

Since you're out of town a few days a week, you
can't get something which requires daily attention.

Obviously.

If I were you I'd get a rat.

Maybe I'll get a hamster.

On layovers, do you touch the hotel bed covers?

I sleep between the sheets.
I wear pajamas and socks.

Good 'cuz they're covered with cum.
I saw it on Forensic Science.

Sometimes when Kimberlie's tired

of answering call lights
and fetching beverages one at a time,
she pretends she's a Stepford wife.

She walks slowly moving her hips
as she smiles, *Of course,*

I'll be right back with that.

She finds it keeps her going.

Turbo

Hamsters are originally from the Middle East. Because they burrow underground during the day and travel by night, they lived unbeknownst to humans for thousands of years. Eventually, sightings were made and rumors began to circulate about the creature. Still, hamsters remained a myth because even though they were sought, humans were unable to discover them for many more years.

Saint Valentine

I won you at the carnival while trying to win a poster of a cat
wearing a suit.

It's that you keep saying you're tired makes me want to weep.
You won't sleep when I ask,
You wish something was yours,
We are poor and I braid your soft hair.

From our rooftop our eyes are turned not upward,
but to the lit window of the pastel building across the street.
A man has been sitting at the window for hours looking one way
down the street.

In a National Park

Dumbarton Oaks is closed—
black metal gate locked.
People pass Kimberlie in pairs
or with dogs.
Lots of trees a bridge grey stone
like the one in ~~Missouri~~ Montana.
Kimberlie is alone too.

Ahhh, someone gasping or singing.
Creek, pink flower floating.
Kimberlie is too alone.
Where is the boy with his white
leash and dog?

She's not pretty but she has an accent

I saw her one time after that. I said that's a nice dress on you,
your arms don't look that fat in it.

Maui, snorkeling

Round. Speckled. Careful.
The puffer fish knows he's being followed.
He swims a little,
turns to face her.
She keeps her distance,
which is about four feet.
He turns his back
and swims a different direction.

They pass a school of fish.
They pass another puffer,
a Moorish idle, needle fish.

And again the little yellow fins slowly
turn the fat brown body.
He looks at her. His eyes shift
then quickly back to her.
She can't help but laugh a little.
Saltwater seeps through the crevice
her cheeks make with the mask,
a bit goes up her nose.
He turns and swims.

You're so far away
How can I

If you come down over the hill
if I'm wearing bells and dancing
if they shine if it's dark out
but the stars you think I am one
I'm fallen
it burns you to touch me
and you love me you
really do

II. Mary

Understanding Mary

People have come to my house
and I have the same smell they said
they saw a fingernail in the soup cup,
black hair and pink on the teeth
of the fork.

Yesterday there were people
cooking in my kitchen
and I could almost smell the food.
I stood in the hallway folding clothes
I thought maybe they'd say something
invite me in perhaps
but they never did.

And I never did plant those seeds.

Years ago I thought of doing it
and I should have because the trees
would be full grown by now
and we'd have plenty of oranges.

Death

Mary and the Angel

I am alone   whispering

                                                    dying

            whispering

I must be dying,
why else am I crumpled on the floor?

                                                    Mary, Mary of ours, Mary

I will get up

                                                    whispering

dying

                                                    whispering

get up to wash the window
behind the kitchen sink

                                                    Mary, Mary of ours, Mary

rising

                                                    faltering

rising

the window washes well

                                                    climbing

someone's at the door

                                                    dying

I run run up
scream in the wind like ice

                                                    For us you lay lay grave

I cannot rest

                                                    alive

I watch her

                                                    above

Kimberlie from Mary's perspective

It's your fault, she says, scraping her nails
on the table. I float back to the wall.

You shouldn't be here anymore you've got to leave.
Is she talking to me?
No one else is in the room.
You've got to leave I said this isn't your house anymore.

This is my house. This is my house
I let her come in here how dare she!

You're not supposed to be here.
There's someplace else you're supposed to be
I don't know why you're waiting.

She has gotten ready for this.
She's pulled the sides of her long hair back.
Her lips are bright red.
She's wearing her high-heeled boots with her long, black skirt.

Kimberlie fingers the white charm on her necklace.
Her torso leans forward and her legs are spread apart.
I think this is part of your tooth, she smiles,
I found it under the sink.

SFO-EWR

(St)Eve:

My friend in LA teases me for being Jewish, I tease him for being Latino.
He called the other night and left this message, *Hello Heather, I just wanted to call and let you know that I'm the Mary, and you're the Jewish princess sitting on the stoop eating cotton candy.*

I called him back I said, *Hello Heather, I just wanted you to know that I'm the Mary and you're the Spanish maid ironing my shirt and making macaroni.*

He said, *No Heather, it's time you finally accept that I'm the Mary, and you're the Rhoda.*

He always thinks he's more popular than me.

Jeff Buckley's "Hallelujah"

I'm tired of her complaining.
I'm tired of the way she looks past the window
not through it.
She's becoming increasingly obsessed with music
and daytime TV: Oprah makes her cry.

Mary doesn't understand that Oprah isn't in the room
anymore than she is and she insists on calling me back
at the commercials' end so I won't miss anything
Oprah has to say.

One time I turned on John Edwards.
She looked slightly confused but mostly bored.

I'm waiting for Oprah to say,
*If you have a secret you need to tell someone
you love write to us.*

Then I'm not sure you can have a secret and
also have love, maybe that's what I'm trying
to tell her.

Interrogating Mary

dark morning light

Mary sits on the floor gleaming against the wall.
She is tightly curled into the fabric of a jagged afghan.
Kimberlie facing her.

one wooden chair

one cup of tea

Mary, what happened to you exactly?

                I'm not sure what you mean.

Something, I think, violent.

                Violet?

Violent.

[*Space and time emerged from Einstein's reworking as malleable constructs whose form and appearance depend on one's state of motion.* Kimberlie has passed days in a number of hours and her skin is holding up quite well despite the dry air.]

Mary tightens the afghan further around her fist.

                What would make you say such a thing?
                (I heard a noise—a sort of rustling—coming
                down the hall.)

[*They can also warp and curve in response to the presence of matter or energy.* Kimberlie likes to tease the preservatives in airplane food is what keeps her looking young.]

Why are you still here?

                    I live here.

I live here now Mary.

                    You visit every couple of days, Kimberlie.
                    I am always here. This is my house you
                    understand.

                    My husband will be home soon.

Kimberlie's painted toenails press into the tiled floor.

I could make you leave if I wanted.

                    I want to look pretty and I want
                    my skin to shine.

III. Recovery

Volatile

Kimberlie feels her duties have risen
and so she deserves a raise. Now she not only has to serve
the meals and drinks, coffee or tea, administer CPR, first aid, defibrillator,
keep saying hello, hang and pass back coats—*hello,*
check on the feature film and connecting flights, *hello,*
feed the cockpit, *hello hello,*
but also be ready to kill any unruly passengers.
She's been planning it out—
hello—it has to do with the ice mallet
and changing jumpseats right after take off
so she can look down the aisle and say hello.

Empathy

Kimberlie's body knows the texture of the space.
Knows too well what it feels like to lean against the wall,
the chair, the carpet.

The fluorescent lights, the still quality of the air.

The shine off the coffeepot handle the engines the screaming styrofoam cups the carpet.

Acute Stress Disorder

Kimberlie lies on the grass at the Civic Center right now smelling human piss.

Cloud.   Cloud.

Big building Big building Big building.

This grassy patch is in a square.
Take comfort in the square.

Prayer

I am not   let me   take in
to see her   there   by the counter
Mary   hold me
remember me Mary   when I leave
when I come   you're there
aren't you   I know
I've been   a little bit strange
I wanted so much   to please

DEN-EWR

September 21, 2001

Kimberlie and the pilot.

Are you afraid to fly now?

> *Do you know the wildebeests on the Discovery Channel?*

No.

> *You know, they get to a place where they have to cross the crocodile infested river and there is no other way to go so they all run across at the same time knowing a few of them will be eaten but the majority of them will make it.*

I'm flying now but I'm frightened.

I'm arranging packets of sugar.

> *Imagine how the wildebeests feel.*

Scenery

There, as here, there are no doors.
The entrance opens to the sky. Opens

to ruin everywhere to crumpled buildings
and dust there, as here, where we're sealed in

and pressurized. It rains tonight.
They think anyone still alive

will drown. This morning they pulled
a flight attendant out

from the wreckage of the Towers
arms still tied behind her back.

The body was intact though the flesh
had partially melted away.

Souvenir

In Narita Kimberlie isn't afraid of the approaching typhoon or the
women with fans and white umbrellas greeting each other as they
wind down the street.

Shops with baskets, computers, samples of pickled vegetables.

Kimberlie eats a brown salted rice cake on a stick.

She has no money. She's thirsty.

School girls with short plaid skirts and leg warmers.

A man presents an English menu and nods.
He has a big smile,
direct eye-contact.

At the temple Kimberlie too puts incense in the cauldron
and brushes the dark smoke over her
forehead over her heart.

She takes off her shoes and kneels before god who is blue,
has three eyes and two fangs.

Employee Email

Hey Cracker,

Did you hear they're laying a bunch of people off. I hope you don't have to go back to stripping. Your ass has gotten big from eating all that glazed chicken and your tits are starting to sag. I don't think you can pull it off anymore. Write when you get a chance.

Love and miss you,
Kimberlie

Flight School

Please, I don't need to know how to take off or land. Just show me how to steer.

Roots

There was
                    a home

    once, remember

                            the wallpaper clocks   now
no home

to go home

            to   happens

    when you move

                a lot

Let me try to explain

When someone's husband leaves them, and they have to go to work
for four consecutive days, they need to talk about it.

Or when someone's sister gets married

or when they have a baby

or leave their baby for the first time.

Two or ten people who've met that day can go out to dinner
and from the laughter and conversation, you'd think they'd known
each other for years.

I was surprised the first time I entered the crew lounge
and saw so many uniformed bodies passed out on couches and chairs.

I was surprised the first time there was something I needed to say.

Donosti
San Sebastian

It's like that time they stole the crop duster and took out parts of LA by spreading a chemical disease and she tried to call Heidi all day. Heidi never answered but suddenly showed up at her door and stayed with her for two months.

Then it was like when they lived in Spain—Heidi did all the cooking because Kimberlie didn't know how. Heidi sat her down at the blue tiled cutting table in the center of the kitchen and had her slice the garlic and onions while she stood at the counter stirring. They didn't have a phone, TV, or radio, but they had lots of wine and cheap cigarettes. They had a deck of cards but Heidi got sick of Old Maid.

One time ETA was shooting fire at the police and they didn't see ETA coming because the streets were tall and narrow and because sometimes people surprise you. As they turned the corner laughing, 30 young men with black ski masks covering their faces were running towards them. Soon they were all running together with the police firing rubber balls at their backs. There was no distinction made for civilians who happened to get in the way.

Weekend Getaway: Big Sur

Generally, you won't see a mountain lion unless a mountain lion wants you to see it.

Always walk loudly so you don't surprise one just in case.

If a mountain lion does become interested in you, raise your hands in the air so you appear larger.

You may want to put a child or a small adult on your shoulders for added height.

Whatever you do, don't crouch down to pick something up or turn around.

Remain facing them.

Don't corner them, always leave them an out.

If a mountain lion attacks, you must counter attack, that is your only chance.

People have been successful at fighting off mountain lions.

You haven't beaten them so much as they decided it wasn't worth it.

It's a good idea to always carry a large stick or a handful of stones.

Tomb

And yet something stays

Falls like stars
                                from the sky

~~thousands of voices~~   hush

                                burning
                                        dust

I'm so glad you're my sister

I can't imagine not having a sister
Not having <u>you</u> as my sister

As if something stays

Decisions

Do you think what happened has changed you?

>My friend volunteered to bring the firemen food. Glass
particles in the air cut her face. What she hated most was
the shoes.

Do you think you have changed?

>I have been afforded the luxury of time to think about it,
and I think if I had to choose between being burned alive or
jumping, I would have jumped too.

What do you want now?

>I want my own home. I want to walk into a familiar smell
and see the faces of people who love me and are happy to see
me. I'd like to have a child and hold it on my lap while
teaching it to read. I'd like soft hair against my cheek.

Hong Kong Ladies' Night Market

3-5-02

Kimberlie sifting through a table of knock-off watches
5 for $100 HK or $12 US

She looks across the alley to Bin Laden
t-shirts displayed on a wall t-shirts

of the twin towers burning, crumbling
a celebration

On the wall directly behind the watches
beaded American flag purses

Kimberlie hasn't slept in over a day and she weaves
through the crowd in the damp night heat

Deviation from the Sonnet: Suspected Witch

After the fire, I found her little teeth
amongst the ashes and the chains I made
a wreath out of her teeth and leaves and bees
to hang around the tombstone of her grave.

I don't believe she committed any crime.
I think the neighbors didn't like her shape
or her bright eyes with their unusual shine
that competed with the sun and dimmed the lake.

The neighbors should fear now—I've cast a spell
even after death they'll hear this bell.

Where do friends come from

Heidi is from Vietnam.
She came over during the war.
Kimberlie is glad because she loves her.
Loves when Heidi is there and she feels more fleshy and full.

Kimberlie gave her a bag of colored marshmallows
for the drive back down to LA.
When you eat the pink ones think of me,
she kissed her on the cheek.

Gypsy

Pretty Jessie has dark wavy hair and full lips.
She loves her ass.
She leaves sticker offerings
on the dashboard of my car.

She came over chewing gum,
a flower in her hair.
I said, "Look what I've done to my room
I've painted it pale blue.
These curtains I found I thought
they were just white
till I died them soft maroon
and all the little stars came out.

"I framed this photo I blew up.
I took it of the Trevi fountain in Rome.
When I was there I threw a coin in as I was told
that would ensure I'd return to Rome one day.

"One week later in Greece my flight canceled.
I had to take the train all the way back
through Italy, southern France,
and over to Spain in order to get back on time.
There were no flights for several days,
it being a Greek holiday and all."

"This is what's fun about being poor,"
Jessie said, moving away from the fish tank.
"If you had money,
 you would have just bought everything
or paid someone else to do it.
When you're poor you have to be magical.
I love your room Kimberlie."

(What can I take from here.
I like to take from her.)

Love Me Forever

Act I
Scene 1

close up on rain

Kimberlie carving a pregnant woman
with wood and a pocket knife

we aren't sure where we are

Often it's dark enough and I don't think I'll be hungry

we aren't afraid to die but that we'll be forgotten

So offer to die a hero,
they'll swear remembrance—Boo—
and you're immortal, some sort of savior

Hallelujah

I like the sound of it

The planes crash during this slow part in the music
and everything gets quiet

Flaming puffs of smoke

It begins again

Lie down now on the white branches

Kimberlie wipes ashes over her forehead
over her heart

Hallelujah   Hallelujah

Amen

Notes

The following texts are referenced in this book of poems:

The Elegant Universe, Brian Greene
W.W. Norton and Co. New York, London, 1999

The Essential Hamster, Betsy Sikora Siino, Ed.
Howell Book House, Hungry Minds, Inc. New York, 1999.

"Hallelujah," by Leonard Cohen, as performed by Jeff Buckley.

FENCEbooks

Sky Girl   Rosemary Griggs   2003 ALBERTA PRIZE

Nota   Martin Corless-Smith

APPREHEND   Elizabeth Robinson
                                                  2003 FENCE MODERN POETS SERIES

Father of Noise   Anthony McCann

The Real Moon of Poetry   Tina Brown Celona
and Other Poems   2002 ALBERTA PRIZE

The Red Bird   Joyelle McSweeney
                                                  2002 FENCE MODERN POETS SERIES

Can You Relax in My House   Michael Earl Craig

ZIRCONIA   Chelsey Minnis   2001 ALBERTA PRIZE

MISS AMERICA   Catherine Wagner

about **FENCE**books

FENCE was launched in the spring of 1998. A biannual journal of poetry, fiction, art and criticism, *Fence* has a mission to redefine the terms of accessibility by publishing challenging writing distinguished by idiosyncrasy and intelligence rather than by allegiance with camps, schools, or cliques. *Fence* has published works by some of the most esteemed contemporary writers as well as excellent writing by completely unknowns. It is part of our mission to support young writers who might otherwise have difficulty being recognized because their work doesn't answer to either the mainstream or to recognizable modes of experimentation.

FENCEbooks is an extension of that mission: With our books we provide exposure to poets and writers whose work is excellent, challenging, and truly original. **The Alberta Prize** is an annual series administered by Fence Books in collaboration with the Alberta duPont Bonsal Foundation. The Alberta Prize offers publication of a first or second book of poems by a woman, as well as a five thousand dollar cash prize.

Our second prize series is the **Fence Modern Poets Series**. This contest is open to poets of either gender and at any stage in their career, and offers a one thousand dollar cash prize in addition to book publication.

For more information about either prize, visit our website at www.fencebooks.com, or send an SASE to: Fence Books/[Name of Prize], 303 East Eighth Street, #B1, New York, New York, 10009.

For more about *Fence,* visit www.fencemag.com.